BIBLICAL
FILTERS
FOR YOUR MEDIA CHOICES
Revised Edition

I0683401

*"Taking every thought captiive
to the obedience of Christ.'
2 Corinthians 10:5*

Joseph Schillero, Jr.

ARPress

ARPress
45 Dan Road Suite 5
Canton MA 02021
Hotline: 1(888) 821-0229
Fax: 1(508) 545-7580

Ordering Information:
Quantity sales. Special discounts are available on quantity purchases by corporations, associations, and others. For details, contact the publisher at the address above.

Printed in the United States of America.

ISBN-13:   Softcover   979-8-89389-028-0
                  eBook   979-8-89389-029-7

Library of Congress Control Number: 2024908916

TABLE OF CONTENTS

INTRODUCTION
HOW'S YOUR HEART?

Keep your heart with all diligence, for out of it spring the issues of life. (Proverbs 4:23)

For the most part I've always been a person who has tried to live a healthy lifestyle. I've usually been one to exercise and eat fairly well. As I grew older and headed into midlife, I realized the importance of taking care of myself even more, especially when it comes to my heart. Did you know that heart disease is the #1 health problem for men and women in the U.S.? If you don't pay attention to diet and exercise, you will probably pay for your lack of discipline with clogged arteries. I believe that God would have us all take care of our bodies in a way that is wise and balanced.

However, I've come to believe that there's a much bigger problem in the U.S. today concerning our hearts. That problem is the condition of our spiritual hearts. Consider the following verses of Scripture:

My son, give attention to my words; incline your ear to my sayings. Do not let them depart from your eyes; keep them in the midst of your heart. (Proverbs 4:20-21)

My son, give me your heart, and let your eyes observe my ways. (Proverbs 23:26)

The light of the eyes rejoices the heart, and a good report makes the bones healthy. (Proverbs 15:30)

As he thinks in his heart so is he. (Proverbs 23:7)

The heart of the wise teaches his mouth, and adds learning to his lips. (Proverbs 16:23)

Out of the abundance of the heart the mouth speaks. (Matthew 12:34)

As in water face reveals face, so a man's heart reveals the man. (Proverbs 27:19)

Man looks at the outward appearance but the LORD looks at the heart. (1 Samuel 16:7)

I would like to emphasize two important truths concerning these nine Scripture verses.

Truth #1 – Out of the heart flow the issues of life

What are the issues of life? The issues of life encompass who we are— our attitudes, desires, affections, pursuits, motives, emotions, and the very words we speak. Proverbs 27:19 says, "As in water face reveals face, so a man's heart reveals the man." If you or I were to look into a perfectly calm pond or lake, we would see a perfect reflection of our face. The water would reveal *who we are*. If God wants to know who we *really* are, He looks into our hearts.

Truth #2 – The mind (the eyes and the ears) is the gateway to the heart

If we really care about the state of our hearts, we will be careful to guard what we allow into our eyes (what we watch) and our ears (what we listen to). The condition of our hearts will be affected by the entertainment and media choices that we make (Galatians 6:8). That is why it is so important to guard our hearts with "all diligence." The word diligence means constant, persevering, effort. Satan never takes a day off when it comes to trying to fill our hearts and minds with lies. As followers of Christ, we must not take one moment off when it comes to guarding our hearts. Unfortunately, many Christians have not only taken time off, they have gone on extended vacations from media discernment. The result of that type of lifestyle is found in Romans 8:6, "To be <u>carnally minded</u> is <u>death</u>...." A dirty heart causes death in our faith, death in our joy, death in our ministries, death in our marriages and families, and death in our relationship with God. Are you guarding your heart with all diligence?

We also find in the New Testament a concern for our thought life. Consider the exhortation by the Apostle Paul in 2 Corinthians 10:5 when he tells us to "take captive every thought to make it obedient to Christ." Before we allow thoughts and images to enter our eyes or ears, we should ask the question, "Am I being obedient to Christ?" When we turn on the TV, go to a movie, watch Netflix or listen to our favorite music, the question that should preface these media choices is, "Am I being obedient to Christ?" If we have accepted Jesus Christ into our hearts as our personal Savior and Lord, being obedient to Him is the litmus test of our love for Him. Jesus said in John 14:15, "If you love Me, keep My commandments."

We've established four important biblical truths:

1) God cares deeply about the state of our hearts

2) The eyes and ears are the gateway to the heart

3) We are to guard our hearts with "all diligence"

4) We are to be obedient to Christ in our thought lives

This all makes sense, but there are still some tough questions to be answered. What are we supposed to keep out of our hearts and what exactly is obedience to Christ when it comes to our thought lives? The booklet in your hand is going to help you to answer these questions.

One of the catch phrases of our ministry is, "Getting people to *think about* what they *think about*." Our goal as a ministry is not to tell you *what* to think but rather to teach you *how* to think. God wants us to think *biblically*. Consider the following verse of Scripture:

His divine power has given to us all things that pertain to life and godliness, through the knowledge of Him who called us by glory and virtue. (2 Peter 1:3)

What a fantastic promise of Scripture! Everything that we need pertaining to life and godliness is found in God and His Word! I believe that "everything" includes the wisdom to make media choices that are pleasing to God. The title of this booklet is *Biblical Filters For Your Media Choices*.

A *filter* is simply something that cleanses an object of impurities. The filters on our furnaces keep dust and dirt out of our lungs. The filters in our cars keep dirt out of our oil. The filters in our swimming pools keep the water pure and clean. The biblical filters in this booklet are designed to keep our hearts pure and clean before God. I have used these teachings in my life and the life of my family for many years. Using these teachings does not guarantee that all of your media choices will be easy. But I guarantee that they will help you to look at your choices from God's perspective. Some choices will be clear as day—black and white. Other choices will be gray and more difficult to discern. However, if the goal of your life is to please our Lord Jesus Christ, the teachings in this booklet will bring you closer to that goal.

As you begin to use these filters, please be mindful that God is not against TV, movies, video games or computers. God is also not against action, adventure, suspense, romance or comedy. God is against media choices that will ultimately harm us, our families, our churches and bring dishonor to His name. GOD IS FOR YOU! He loves you and wants to bless your life. These teachings are not designed to take *good things* away from you. They are designed to fill your life with the joy and peace that comes with obeying God and walking in His Word. I pray that these teachings will bring conviction, repentance and restoration to your life, your family and the body of Christ.

By His grace,
Joe Schillero Jr.

BIBLICAL FILTERS FOR YOUR
MEDIA CHOICES

Biblical Filter #1 – Are my media choices taking up too much of my time?

Biblical Filter #2 – Are my media choices encouraging me to worship someone or something other than God?

Biblical Filter #3 – Is the central theme or message of my media choice positive?

Biblical Filter #4 – Has my media choice influenced me to sin against God?

Biblical Filter #5 – Will my media choice bring temptation into my life?

Biblical Filter #6 – What does my media choice say about the value of other people?

Biblical Filter #7 – Will my media choice desensitize my view of evil?

Biblical Filter #8 – Would I want others following the example of my media choices?

Biblical Filter #9 – Am I asking the right questions about my media choices?

Biblical Filter #10 – Am I glorifying God through my media choices?

"So teach us to number our days that we may gain a heart of wisdom."

(Psalm 90:12)

BIBLICAL FILTER #1

Are my media choices taking up too much of my time?

Even if the content of all our media choices is good, we still need to ask ourselves the above question. We are all given twenty-four hours in each day. As followers of the Lord Jesus Christ, we need to prioritize our lives based on loving and serving Christ and others. In Ephesians 5:16, God talks about *"redeeming the time, because the days are evil."* What are we doing with our time each day? Are we just spending it or are we investing it? Are we spending ample time reading and studying the precious Word of God? Are we sharing God's Word with lost people? Are we serving in our local churches? Are we making sure that our families (spouses and children) are given their proper priorities in our lives? I don't believe that God is against recreation or entertainment. I believe that they can be a part of a balanced Christian life. However, if these things take up an inordinate amount of time in our lives, we are probably not making the Kingdom of God a priority in our lives. Won't you pray today and ask God to show you where you're spending too much time on media? It could be too much TV, too much time playing video games, checking social media, or being glued to our cell phones. Remember, it's not that these things are necessarily bad; it's all about balance based on biblical priorities.

Only one life will soon be past; only what's done for Christ will last. (C.T. Studd)

QUESTIONS TO PONDER

1) Does silence bother me? (Can God speak to my heart when there is constant noise?)

2) Is it possible that I may actually be addicted to some of my media choices? What steps can I take to break these addictions?

3) Am I spending my time or investing my time?
   Does the majority of my time have eternal significance?

*"I will praise You with my whole heart;
before the gods I will sing praises to You."*

(Psalm 138:1)

BIBLICAL FILTER #2

Are my media choices encouraging
me to worship someone or
something else other than God?

What comes to your mind when you think of the word "worship"? Several descriptive words come to my mind. I think of passion, love, devotion, honor and service. To worship someone or something would involve all of these.

Who or what are you *passionate* about? Who or what do you truly *love*? Who or what do you *admire*, *honor* and *serve*? We can attach these words to many people or things in our lives. To whomever or whatever we attach these words, there will be a commitment of *time* and *effort*. Who but God Almighty Himself deserves our most dedicated and committed *time* and *effort*? Consider the following verses of Scripture:

"You shall have no other gods before Me." (Exodus 20:3)

For where your treasure is, there your heart will be also. (Matthew 6:21)

Is God the *ultimate* treasure of your life? Is He the recipient of your greatest passion, love, devotion, time and service? If He is the #1 priority in our lives, then our hearts, our time and our efforts will prove this reality. The sad truth for many of us is that *media* has become our god and *media* receives our ultimate worship. How many of us are more passionate about our favorite Sunday football game than about worship on Sunday morning? We scream and shout over a leather ball being thrown up and down the field, yet we are ashamed to raise our hands in church. How many of us loathe our church's prayer meetings, yet we'll plan our entire week around our favorite sitcoms, soap operas, or Netflix series. Often, we have very little time for God during the week, but somehow we find time to log twenty or more hours per week playing video games or checking social media statuses. Something is definitely wrong with this reality. There is nothing inherently wrong with football, TV, video games or many other forms of media. The question we need to ask ourselves is found in Mathew 6:33. Are we seeking first God's kingdom and righteousness or have we allowed media to be our god and priority?

<u>QUESTIONS TO PONDER</u>

1) What form of media entertainment am I more passionate about than God?

2) What are some steps that I can take to adjust my priorities?

"And do not be conformed to this world, but be transformed by the renewing of your mind, that you may prove what is that good and acceptable and perfect will of God."

(Romans 12:2)

BIBLICAL FILTER #3

*Is the central theme or message of
my media choice positive?*

Our mental and spiritual ingestion of today's media can be equated to a healthy lifestyle of eating and drinking. I'm sure you've heard the old saying, "You are what you eat." The healthier the food is, the healthier you will be. To benefit from a healthy diet, the *majority* of what you eat and drink must be healthy. Eating healthy food 50% of the time and eating junk food the other 50% of the time will not make you a healthy person. However, our bodies can tolerate a *little bit* of junk food if the bulk of what we're eating is good. In drawing this analogy to our spiritual life, I am not implying that a *little bit* of sin or compromise is ever *spiritually* healthy. I do believe that there are TV programs, movies, music, and video games that have central themes or messages that are primarily *good*, but also present some negative or sinful aspects.

For example, there may be a movie that is filled with positive messages about family, faith, friendship and forgiveness, but one of the main characters is an adulterer and drunkard. Adultery and drunkenness are both sinful and wrong. But, if they are portrayed in a way that teaches the consequences of such behavior and doesn't glorify such behavior, they may be acceptable in a movie. If a movie is *filled* with adultery and drunkenness as a primary theme with no consequences and used primarily to entertain the flesh, I would then say that the movie is probably unhealthy to our spiritual well-being.

Many people will watch and justify their unhealthy viewing by the fact that there were a *few* positive aspects to it.

I would equate that thinking to eating out of a garbage dumpster. Most of the garbage would probably be rotten and inedible. However, you would be able to find something in the dumpster that you could eat that had nutritional value. A person who cares about their health would not be eating out of a garbage dumpster. A person who cares about his or her spiritual health will not partake in the vast majority of today's R-rated movies, sitcoms, Top 40 music and violent video games. I love the following Scripture verse as a reference source for what we *should* be listening to and watching.

> **Whatever things are <u>true</u>, whatever things are <u>noble</u>, whatever things are <u>just</u>, whatever things are <u>pure</u>, whatever things are <u>lovely</u>, whatever things are of <u>good report</u>, if there is any <u>virtue</u> and if there is anything <u>praiseworthy</u> – <u>meditate</u> on these things. (Philippians 4:8)**

What a great and practical list that we can use when filtering our media choices! I have found that when I use this list as my reference in my decision making, I feel so much better after participating in my media choices. When I've walked out of a movie that has central themes that are *noble, virtuous* and *praiseworthy*, I usually feel uplifted and inspired. When I've viewed a movie or TV program that is filled with violence, sex, murder or other negative themes, I usually walk away feeling depressed and down.

Somehow, I have the idea that God is *for us* and *not against us* when it comes to us enjoying our media choices with the emotions with which He has blessed us. Let's trust Him and His Word today as our filter for making positive media choices.

QUESTIONS TO PONDER

1) Write down some of the media choices that you have recently made and filter them through Philippians 4:8. Would you consider them *healthy* to your spiritual life in Christ?

2) How did you feel after attending your last movie or playing your last video game? Did you feel uplifted or depressed? Even if you felt good, do you think that you were feeding the *flesh* or the *spirit*?

3) What are some media choices that you believe you should give up?

"For the death that He died, He died to sin once for all; but the life that He lives, He lives to God. Likewise you also, reckon yourselves to be dead indeed to sin, but alive to God in Christ Jesus our Lord."

(Romans 6:10-11)

BIBLICAL FILTER #4

Has my media choice influenced me to sin against God?

There's really nothing complicated about this question. Have my choices of TV programs, movies, music, video games, or internet sites caused me to sin? Has my favorite sitcom provoked me to laugh at off- color jokes? Has my favorite song on the radio provoked rebellion in my heart toward authority? Has my favorite video game made me a more aggressive and violent person? Has my favorite internet site provoked me to sexual lust? If we truly love God, we will care about the answers to these and other questions concerning sin and our media choices. If we truly love God, the Bible says that we will keep His commandments.

"If you love Me, keep My commandments." (John 14:15)

None of us is ever going to be sinless. The only sinless person to walk on this earth was Jesus Christ Himself. However, to have no regard for sin when it comes to our media choices (or any choices for that matter) is inconsistent with what the Bible teaches about being a follower of Jesus Christ. In fact, if you really want to know God's view of sin, consider the following verse of Scripture:

If your right eye causes you to sin, pluck it out and cast it from you; for it is more profitable for you that one of your members perish, than for your whole body to be cast into hell. And if your right hand causes you to sin, cut it off and cast it from you; for it is more profitable for you that one of your members perish, than for your whole body to be cast into hell. (Matthew 5:29-30)

In some of the biblical counseling courses that I have taken, this verse has been referred to as a "radical amputation." One of my relatives had to have the bottom portion of his leg amputated. It was a devastating decision for him to make. However, he felt that he had no choice. It was a decision of his *leg* or his *life*. God knows the powerful negative influence that sin will have on our lives for both now and eternity.

> **Do not be deceived: God cannot be mocked. A man reaps what he sows. The one who sows to please his sinful nature, from that nature will reap destruction; the one who sows to please the Spirit, from the Spirit will reap eternal life. (Galatians 6:7-8)**

> **Those who live according to the flesh set their minds on the things of the flesh, but those who live according to the Spirit, the things of the Spirit. For to be carnally minded is <u>death,</u> but to be spiritually minded is life and peace. (Romans 8:5-6)**

God knows that if we choose to be "spiritually minded" it will produce "life and peace." God loves us and wants that for us. If we choose to be "carnally minded" we choose "death." For some of us that may mean death in our marriages, families, or other relationships. And for some of us that may even mean eternal death. If you choose to reject Jesus Christ because of your love of *sin*, you reject the only means of salvation.

> **Jesus said to him, "I am the way, the truth, and the life. No one comes to the Father except through Me." (John 14:6)**

The verses in Matthew 5:29-30 tell us that there is no amount of pleasure in sin that will be worth the consequences—in this life or the life to come. If you know Jesus Christ as your Lord and Savior, bad media choices will not send you to hell. Jesus took your punishment on Calvary. However, bad media choices will steal your joy, replace it with sorrow, and make you unfruitful for the kingdom of God.

QUESTIONS TO PONDER

1)   Make a list of your most popular media choices (TV, movies, video games, music, Internet). Have any of these media choices influenced you to sin against God?

2)   If social media, your favorite music artist, or internet site has influenced you to sin, are you willing to give them up? Are you willing to go through a "radical amputation" for Jesus?

"Watch and pray, lest you enter into temptation. The spirit indeed is willing, but the flesh is weak."
(Mathew 26:41)

BIBLICAL FILTER #5

*Will my media choice bring
temptation into my life?*

Biblical Filter #5 takes us to an even deeper commitment than #4. Biblical Filter #4 challenged us with the question, "Has my media choice influenced me to sin?" Our next filter challenges us with the question, "Is it even *tempting* me to sin?" You may not be looking at pornography at the present moment, but are you constantly struggling in your thought life because of some of the images you're seeing on TV or the internet? You may not be *physically* hurting other people presently, but are you becoming more aggressive and impatient with other people because of the video games you're playing? You may not have committed adultery, but has your favorite soap opera or TV show caused you to think about the possibility? You may not have sinned *yet*, but trust me, Satan is very patient. He will continue to feed your flesh and work on your weakness until you give in; if you choose to let him! Consider the following verses of Scripture:

A prudent man foresees evil and hides himself, but the simple pass on and are punished. (Proverbs 22:3)

Put on the Lord Jesus Christ, and make no provision for the flesh, to fulfill its lusts. (Romans 13:14)

Lead us not into temptation, but deliver us from the evil one. (Matthew 6:13)

The principle in all three of these Scripture verses is clear. A wise follower of the Lord Jesus Christ will not only strive to *not sin*, he will also strive to not even be *tempted* to sin. In fact, I believe that the prayer in Matthew 6:13 expresses this exact sentiment. "Lead us not into temptation but deliver us from the evil one." We should be asking God, in prayer, to not only protect us from sin, but also from even the *possibility* of sinning. When we have this attitude, we can be sure that we're walking in the "fear of the Lord" and a love for God.

> **There hath no temptation taken you but such as is common to man: but God is faithful, who will not suffer you to be tempted above that ye are able; but will with the temptation also make a way to escape, that ye may be able to bear it. (1 Corinthians 10:13)**

QUESTIONS TO PONDER

1)   What current media selections in your life are tempting you to sin? What are the temptations?

      How close are you to committing these sins?

2)   What media choices would be wise for you to give up based on the principles of this teaching?

"In this is love, not that we loved God, but that He loved us and sent His Son to be the propitiation for our sins. Beloved, if God so loved us, we also ought to love one another."

(1 John 4:10-11)

BIBLICAL FILTER #6

What does the media choice say about the value of other people?

"Do to others as you would have them do to you."(Luke 6:31)

Love the Lord your God with all your heart and with all your soul and with all your strength and with all your mind; and love your neighbor as yourself. (Luke 10:27)

How do you think other people should be treated? One common sense litmus test is to ask ourselves, "How do I want to be treated?" Usually, the answer to the second question will take care of the answer to the first question. That is why God tells us in Luke 10:27, "Love your neighbor as yourself." Often times this verse of Scripture is used as an exhortation for people to "love themselves." However, the verse is actually an exhortation for us to "love others." It is assumed in the verse that we already "love ourselves." In what way do we "love ourselves?" As a general rule, each and every one of us cares about ourselves. We feed ourselves; we clothe ourselves; we protect ourselves. In a nutshell, we value ourselves. I believe that this type of 'self love' is instinctively put into all of us. I do not believe that this verse is a teaching on self-esteem. This verse actually exhorts us to esteem God and to love others. I believe that all people have value and worth and should be treated with love and care . . . just as we love and care for ourselves. All people should be treated with human dignity. The Bible tells us in Psalm 139:14 that we are "fearfully and wonderfully made." All people have value and worth because God loves them and He created them in His image (Genesis 1:26). In fact, He so loves us, that He gave His only begotten Son to die in our place on a cross (John 3:16).

As in all of our thinking processes, we want to think with the "mind of Christ." This means that *our* thoughts should be in agreement with *Jesus's* thoughts. If Jesus values people, we should value people in the same way. How are people being treated in your media choices? If a music artist is singing about the beauty of love and marriage, that artist is showing respect for the institution of marriage and the importance of [being] husband and wife. If your favorite rapper is singing about having sex with a girl in his back seat or raping a girl on his couch, what value is he putting on women? A police officer kills a criminal in the line of duty on your favorite TV show. This action shows the need for justice in our society. One of your favorite video games (e.g., *Grand Theft Auto*) depicts a criminal who kills police officers and has sex with prostitutes to further the game. What value does this game put on the lives of police officers and women who have been shamed by prostitution? What if that Police Officer was your brother or your father? What if that woman in the rap song was your sister or your mother? Would you want them to be treated in this derogatory way?

You may say, "I know that the rapper and video game characters are not "loving their neighbors as themselves," but it's [just] entertainment to me." I would respond with the fact that *Jesus Christ would never entertain himself with such thoughts and images, so neither should we.* Why would we want to fill our hearts and minds with such garbage? Why would we want to give our money (really God's money) to support those who create such ungodly media? If we are followers of the Lord Jesus Christ, we will make media choices that encourage [true biblical love] toward the people that are being depicted.

> **For you were once darkness, but now you are light in the Lord. Walk as children of light (for the fruit of the Spirit is in all goodness, righteousness, and truth), finding out what is acceptable to the Lord. And have no fellowship with the unfruitful works of darkness, but rather expose them. For it is shameful even to speak of those things which are done by them in secret. (Ephesians 5:8-12)**

QUESTIONS TO PONDER

1) Think of some of the characters that are in your favorite TV shows, movies and video games. What value is given to those characters? Does Jesus have that same view of those people? Should you have that view of those people?

2) What media choices do you think you may want to give up based on this biblical filter?

"Be alert and of sober mind. Your enemy the devil prowls around like a roaring lion looking for someone to devour"

(1 Peter 5:8)

BIBLICAL FILTER #7

Will my media choice
desensitize my view of evil?

One dictionary defines desensitize with the following definition: "*To make emotionally insensitive or unresponsive, as by long exposure or repeated shocks.*"

Have you become emotionally insensitive to sin? Have you become unresponsive to sin? Have you allowed yourself to be exposed to sin for long periods of time? If so, you have probably been desensitized to evil. As followers of Jesus Christ, God wants us to have His heart and His attitude toward sin and evil. Rather than being insensitive to sin, it should bother us in our lives and the lives of others. Rather than being unresponsive to sin, we should be proactive towards stopping it. We should be grieving over evil in our life and the lives of others and seeking to repent from it. Our problem is that many of us are the proverbial *frog in the frying pan*. Satan has us cooking in a pot of lukewarm water that is slowly growing hotter and we don't know or care that we're being cooked. We become desensitized because we are *sinful*; we choose to expose our hearts and minds to things that God warns against or forbids. If you are constantly watching chick flicks that portray pre-marital sex as normal and acceptable, you may no longer be bothered by the following verses of Scripture:

> **Therefore put to death your members which are on the earth: fornication, uncleanness, passion, evil desire, and covetousness, which is idolatry. Because of these things the wrath of God is coming upon the sons of disobedience. (Colossians 3:5-6)**

For this you know, that no <u>fornicator, unclean</u> person, nor covetous man, who is an idolater, has any inheritance in the kingdom of Christ and God. Let no one deceive you with empty words, for because of these things the wrath of God comes upon the sons of disobedience. (Ephesians 5:5-6)

If you are constantly watching sitcoms and laughing at off-color humor, you may no longer be bothered by these Scripture verses:

Let no corrupt communication proceed out of your mouth, but what is good for necessary edification, that it may impart grace to the hearers. (Ephesians 4:29)

Nor should there be obscenity, foolish talk or coarse joking, which are out of place, but rather thanksgiving. (Ephesians 5:4)

We become desensitized because we are constantly exposing ourselves to lies that are contrary to God's Word. Our hearts are no longer sensitive to the things of God. We may not even realize that we are no longer living our christian lives in the Spirit, but rather that we are living in the flesh. Romans 12:2 exhorts us, "Do not be conformed to this world, but be transformed by the renewing of your mind." Many of us are being *conformed* rather than *transformed*. If we are living in this condition, we are not living a life that is pleasing to God. We also will not be experiencing the fruit of the Spirit: love, joy, peace, patience, kindness, goodness, faithfulness, gentleness and self-control (Galatians 5:22-23). Instead, we will only be experiencing the short-lived fleshly pleasures that many of today's media choices bring us. If you are the *frog in the frying pan* at this very moment, be thankful that God has put this teaching into your path. He loves you and does not want to see you go down a path of destruction.

Do not be deceived, God is not mocked; for whatever a man sows, that he will also reap. For he who sows to his flesh will of the flesh reap corruption, but he who sows to the Spirit will of the Spirit reap everlasting life.

(Galatians 6:7-8)

In my many years as a follower of Jesus Christ, my experience tells me that if you are the *frog in the frying pan* you may not know it; and if you do know it, you may not care. I speak from personal experience as well as observation. God in His love will often put convicting preaching or teaching in our paths to get our attention. If we choose to ignore His Word, He may allow trials in our lives to get our attention. Why does He go to such lengths? Because He understands the truth of Proverbs 27:20, "Hell and destruction are never full; so the eyes of man are never satisfied." Our heavenly Father knows that our sinful natures will never get enough of sin. If He doesn't detour us, we will continue down a road of destruction in our state of desensitization. The Bible describes us as sheep—"We like sheep have gone astray" (Isaiah 53:6a). Thankfully, we have a loving Shepherd who is constantly pursuing us and leading us in the right direction. Will you heed His still small voice today?

QUESTIONS TO PONDER

1) Make a list of your media choices. Make a list of sins that are present in these choices. How do you feel about these sins? Do they bother you in your life or the lives of others?

2) What steps will you take to become *sensitized* again to the things of God?

"Imitate me, just as I also imitate Christ."
(1 Corinthians 11:1)

BIBLICAL FILTER #8

Would I want others following the example of my media choices?

Once we have trusted in Jesus Christ as our Lord and Savior, one of the primary goals of being a Christian is to conform to the image of Christ (Romans 8:29). Jesus Christ is the ultimate role model. All that God would desire for anyone to be can be found in the life of Christ. Of course, none of us will ever live the perfect, sinless life Jesus lived. However, because of our love for Him, we should strive to be like Him in every way. The Apostle Paul understood this truth; that is why he exhorted the believers in Philippi with the following verse of Scripture:

The things which you learned and received and heard and <u>saw in me</u>, these do, and the God of peace will be with you. (Philippians 4:9)

Paul not only exhorted people to do what he taught, but he also exhorted them to do what they *saw* him do. Paul knew what it meant to lead by *example*. The area that I have been challenged in is being an example to my children. I raised seven children who watched my every move (Trust me, we lived in a small house where there was nowhere to hide.). The greatest tool that I had when it came to raising them was not my words but my example.

Once again, none of us will ever be perfect. Certainly don't let your imperfections keep you from teaching your family the Word of God. However, let's also not be hypocrites when it comes to our lifestyles. We shouldn't be viewing immoral sitcoms while we're telling our kids not to watch them. We can't be viewing R-rated movies while lecturing our kids not to see them. We shouldn't be watching extremely violent shows while exhorting our kids to shut off violent video games. I once heard an extremely convicting sermon on the radio concerning these issues. In a nutshell, the preacher said that whatever lifestyle we were consistently living would probably be duplicated by our children. Wow! Talk about conviction! When I heard that message, I realized that there were media choices that I was making that I definitely wouldn't want my children making. Through the prompting of the Holy Spirit, I did some serious repenting of those choices. As followers of Jesus Christ, we all need to be mindful of the example we're demonstrating to other people. You may not have children, but someone is always watching your life. We're the only Jesus some will ever see!

QUESTIONS TO PONDER

1) Can you think of any media choices in your life where you're being a bad example to your friends, co-workers or family members?

2) Are you willing to give these up to become more like Jesus?

"The fear of the Lord is the beginning of wisdom, and knowledge of the Holy One is understanding."

(Proverbs 9:10)

BIBLICAL FILTER #9

Am I asking the right question
about my media choices?

You shall love the Lord your God with all your heart, with all your soul, and with all your mind. (Matthew 22:37)

In Matthew 22, Jesus quotes this verse from Deuteronomy 6. It is the sum total of all of the commandments in the Bible. The bottom line in our spiritual lives is simply *loving God with passion*. Do we love God? If we do, then all of our decision making will reflect that love— *including our media choices*. Consider the following two questions. Which one applies to your media choices?

1) **How much sex, violence and profanity can I see and hear without it affecting me?**

2) **Am I loving and fearing God with all of my heart, soul, mind and strength in my media choices?**

If Question #1 applies to us, it would seem that the passion of our heart is not God, but rather our media choices. If Question #1 applies to us, we may be more interested in the pleasure that our media choices bring us than we are in staying away from the negative influences of sex, violence and profanity. I'm not saying that Question #1 does not have some legitimacy in our media discernment. I believe that there can be some negative aspects to our choices that do not necessarily negate the big picture of our choice. However, Question #1 may be equated to someone asking, "How close to the edge of a cliff can I get before I risk falling off the edge?" I would ask, "Is the thrill worth the risk involved?"

Question #2 seems to focus on our love and worship of God *more* than our media choices. It's not that our media choices don't matter. It's just that loving and fearing God takes precedence over the fun, excitement or relaxation that our media choices may bring us. Question #2 could be equated to someone asking, "How far away from the edge of the cliff should I stay to keep myself safe from danger?" Question #2 is not only an act of love and worship toward God; it is also an act of wisdom. The same God who we are called to love with all of our heart, soul, mind and strength, loves us more than we could ever imagine. Because He loves us, He wants what is best for us in every area of life, including our media choices. I believe that Question #1 is the *wrong question* to ask. Question #2 is the *right question* to be asking.

If we *really* love God, we will want to please Him in all of our media choices. Think about this. Every time that you are tempted to disobey God in the area of media, you have an opportunity to show Him that you love Him. When you are watching a sitcom and the humor becomes offensive, you can continue to watch, or you can obey God and shut off the TV. When you're driving down the road listening to your radio and a popular song comes on that contradicts your biblical values, you can continue to listen or you can show God that you love Him by shutting the radio off. You may be at a friend's house and he pops in an extremely violent video game that you know is not acceptable to play. You can play it anyway or show God that you love Him by declining to play. Our choices will determine the state of our hearts concerning our love for God. How's your heart today?

QUESTIONS TO PONDER

1)   Do you love God? Have you accepted Jesus Christ into your life as your Lord and Savior?

2)   Make a list of your most popular media choices (TV, movies, video games, music, internet sites). Do these choices reflect a love and fear of God?

3)   Have you forsaken your "first love" for the pleasure of some media entertainment? If so, ask God to forgive you. Seek His strength to repent and sin no more. He loves you!

"For you were bought at a price;
therefore glorify God in your body
and in your spirit, which are God's."

(1 Corinthians 6:20)

BIBLICAL FILTER #10

*Am I glorifying God through
my media choices?*

The chief end of man is to glorify God and enjoy Him forever. (Westminster Catechism)

Therefore, whether you eat or drink, or whatever you do, do all to the glory of God.

(1 Corinthians 10:31)

The ultimate goal of all of our media choices and of all of our lives is to *glorify God*. God is "the Alpha and the Omega, the Beginning and the End" of all things. (Revelation 1:8) "For by Him all things were created that are in heaven and that are on earth, visible and invisible, whether thrones or dominions or principalities or powers. All things were created through Him and for Him." (Colossians 1:16) Everything and anything that is good in our lives must be accredited to *who God is* and what *He* has done. "Shall the ax boast itself against him who chops with it? Or shall the saw exalt itself against him who saws with it? As if a rod could wield itself against those who lift it up, or as if a staff could lift up, as if it were not wood!" (Isaiah 10:15) God deserves the glory for everything in our lives. I believe to glorify God is to draw people's attention to His works and His character. I once heard a sermon on what it means to "glorify God." The preacher described the glory of God with the description of the mantel in his living room. He described it something like this:

The mantel in someone's house is usually above the fireplace and right in the middle of the room. I don't think that I have ever seen an empty mantel. Mantels are always filled with pictures, statues, mementos, etc. What is the purpose of all of these items? Their purpose is to make the mantel look good. They glorify and bring attention to the mantel. It's not that the individual items have no significance in themselves. It's just that their primary purpose is to make the mantel look good. In the same way, the things that we say, the way that we look, the things that we do, should draw attention to God. The goal of our lives is not to draw attention to ourselves; rather, it is to draw attention to God. When people see our lives, they should be thinking, "Their God sure looks good in them!"

Let your light so shine before men, that they may see your good works and <u>glorify</u> your Father in heaven. (Matthew 5:16)

When people look at your life and mine, do you think they're saying, "Their God sure looks good in them?" When they view our media choices, do you think they're saying, "Their God sure looks good in them?" Think about that for a moment. If someone walked into your house and saw you watching your favorite sitcom or soap opera, what would they be thinking about God *in you*? What do you think people are saying about God *in you* when they see you walking into an R-rated movie? What do your friends think about God *in you* when you're spending hours and hours killing people in your favorite video game? Are we glorifying God in our media choices? Are people seeing qualities in our lives that would point them to <u>who God is</u> and <u>what He has done</u> in our lives? Remember, the Bible says that as followers of Jesus Christ we are to be "sanctified." It means to be "set apart." Our lives should be distinctly different from the lives of our unsaved friends. Our values, our words, our conduct and sometimes even our media choices should be different than theirs if we're holding a biblical worldview. One day, we will all stand before God and give an account of our lives. Let's make sure that we can say that our media choices brought glory to the only one who is worthy of glory—our great God and Savior, Jesus Christ.

<u>QUESTIONS TO PONDER</u>

1)   What media choices in your life are not glorifying God?

2)   Do you think that all of our media choices have to be Christian to glorify Him?

3)   How can clean, wholesome, secular media choices glorify God?

*"I call heaven and earth as witnesses today
against you, that I have set before you life and
death, blessing and cursing; therefore choose
life, that both you and your descendants may live."*

(Deuteronomy 30:19)

FINAL THOUGHTS

I hope that you have been challenged by these biblical filters. They are certainly not meant to be an exhaustive study on the subject of media discernment. They are meant to get you thinking about this important subject and to also open up some conversations with your family, youth group or Bible study group. Although I am passionate about helping people to THINK ABOUT what they THINK ABOUT, I am even more passionate about helping people have a relationship with the Lord Jesus Christ. Knowing Jesus and trusting in Him for salvation is the first step in having media discernment. The Bible tells us, "The fear of the Lord is the beginning of wisdom and the knowledge of the Holy One is understanding" (Proverbs 9:10). In this booklet I've shared a considerable amount of information concerning our hearts. Consider the following verses of Scripture. They reveal some sobering characteristics concerning my heart and yours before we accept Jesus as our Savior.

> **"And you He made alive, who were <u>dead in trespasses and sins</u>, in which you once walked according to the course of this world, according to the prince of the power of the air, the spirit who now works in the <u>sons of disobedience</u>, among whom also we all once conducted ourselves in the lusts of our flesh, fulfilling the desires of the flesh and of the mind, and were by nature <u>children of wrath</u>, just as the others." (Ephesians 2:1-3)**

> **"The heart is <u>deceitful</u> above all things, and <u>desperately wicked</u>; who can know it?" (Jeremiah 17:9)**

> **"For <u>all have sinned</u> and <u>fall short</u> of the glory of God."**
> **(Romans 3:23)**

Please consider some of the words and statements that have been underlined. The bible describes us as dead in trespasses and sins, sons of disobedience, children of wrath, deceitful, desperately wicked. I bet your self-esteem is not soaring at this point. Neither is mine! The Gospel of Jesus Christ is referred to as the 'Good News.' However, before you can enjoy the 'Good News' you have to embrace the 'Bad News.' The bad news is that all of us have sinned and fall short of God's holy standard. One day each and every one of us will stand before God in judgment and He will require 100% righteousness and holiness from us (Acts 17:31). The bad news is that none of us can meet that standard. The only person to ever meet that standard was the Lord Jesus Christ. Because God is holy, there must be a just payment for sin. No amount of good works, church attendance, sacraments or media discernment will ever be able to pay for our sin. On our own, we all stand lost and hopeless without God (Ephesians 2:12).

For the first 18 years of my life I would have considered myself a religious and good person. I never had any problem admitting that I was a sinner. I just never believed that I was sinful enough to go to Hell. Hell was for murders and rapists. I wasn't one of those. I considered myself 'good' because my standard for pleasing God was 'the murderers and rapists.' I was certainly better than them. In fact I could think of multitudes of people that weren't as 'good' as me. I came to see that this flawed theology was not true. I believed that the standard of righteousness was 'others.' I'm convinced that a great number of people today also believe this flawed theology. I was very surprised when I found out (through reading the bible) that God Himself was the standard of righteousness. I found out that I had to be as holy as God to enter into heaven. When the reality of this truth hit me I was humbled by the reality of my sinfulness. I came to realize that I was a GREAT sinner and that nothing I could do was going to wash me clean of my unrighteousness. I had embraced the BAD NEWS! I was now ready to also embrace the GOOD NEWS!

"For God so loved the world that He gave His only begotten Son, that whoever believes in Him should not perish but have everlasting life." (John 3:16)

God is a holy God but He is also a God of love! He does not want anyone to go to hell to pay for their sins. In His great love He made a way for us. Jesus Christ the son of God paid for our sins on the cross so that we could be free from the penalty of sin.

"For the wages of sin is death, but the gift of God is eternal life in Christ Jesus our Lord." (Romans 6:23)

Imagine if you would, being convicted of an awful crime. You get arrested, you go to court and the jury finds you GUILTY! You then stand before a judge for your just sentencing. The judge sentences you to death by lethal injection. You are carted off to a room to receive your just punishment. As you lay on the table contemplating your circumstances, you know that you are guilty and deserve what is happening to you. There is no hope! Just before the executioner puts the needle in your arm to end your life, the door swings open and someone yells WAIT! To everyone's surprise it is the judge who sentenced you. He says, "I love this man and I am going to take his punishment." They unstrap you and strap the judge to the table. He receives the injection and dies while you walk out of the building a free man. You receive a pardon that you did not deserve and the judge receives a death that he did not deserve.

"For Christ also suffered once for sins, the just for the unjust, that He might bring us to God." (1 Peter 3:18)

This is a human illustration of God's amazing grace and love. Over 2000 years ago the creator and Lord of the universe became a man and died on a cross to pay for our sins. He took all of our punishment on the cross so that we would not have to pay for our sins in Hell. Some theologians call this the 'Great Exchange.' Jesus takes all of our sins and we get all of His righteousness. This is the GOOD NEWS of the Gospel! What must you and I do to receive God's indescribable gift? (2 Corinthians 9:15)

You must first confess to God that you are a sinner and that no amount of your self-effort will ever be able to pay for your sins.

"For by grace you have been saved through faith, and that not of yourselves; it is the gift of God, not of works, lest anyone should boast." (Ephesians 2:8-9)

Once you've acknowledged your helplessness and hopelessness before God you must then believe on the Lord Jesus Christ. You must believe that He took the punishment for your sins through His death and that He rose from the dead to bring you eternal life.

"If you confess with your mouth the Lord Jesus and believe in your heart that God has raised Him from the dead, you will be saved." (Romans 10:9)

It's that's simple! Jesus asks you to trust in Him through 'faith.' In fact, Jesus exhorts us to come to Him with the "simple faith of a child" (Mark 10:13-16). You may have been a religious person your whole life but you have never trusted in Jesus for your salvation. You may have believed that you must obey a list of rules and regulations to pay for you sins. The Good News and the simple message of Christianity is that Jesus already paid the price. All you must do is repent of your sin and put your trust in Him.

If God's spirit has humbled you at this moment and you have come to see the greatness of your sin and the greatness of Jesus to save you, I would encourage you to pray this prayer:

"Dear God, I confess to you that I am a great sinner. I have fallen short of your standards of righteousness and holiness. I stand guilty before you. I confess my belief that your son Jesus Christ took upon Himself my sins when He died on the cross. I believe that He rose from the dead so that my sins could be forgiven and I could have eternal life. I put all of my trust in His work on the cross for my salvation. I turn from my sin to follow You. Thank you Lord for this free gift of salvation. Amen."

If you have sincerely prayed this prayer the Bible proclaims that you are now a child of God (John 1:12). Your sins have been forgiven and Christ's righteousness has been put on your eternal account. The bible states that you have been JUSTIFIED before God (Romans 5:1). This means that even though you have sinned greatly, God DECLARES you righteous because of what Jesus had done on the cross. God's payment for your sins has been satisfied (1 John 2:1). You are forgiven! But, you must also know that you are more than forgiven; you are a NEW PERSON. The Bible joyfully proclaims that if anyone is 'in Christ,' he is a new creation; old things have passed away; behold, all things have become new.

THINGS TO DO IF YOU ARE A NEW CHRISTIAN

- Begin reading the Bible. "As newborn babes in Christ, desire the pure milk of God's word, that you may grow." (1 Peter 2:2)

- Begin talking to God through prayer. Get to know your heavenly Father. (Mathew 6:9-13).

- Attend a bible-believing church which exalts Jesus as the only way of salvation. (Hebrews 10:24-25)

- Obey Jesus' command and be baptized (Mathew 28:19)

If you have trusted in Jesus as your Savior while reading this booklet we would love to hear from you. We would love to help assist you in your spiritual growth.

God bless you,

Joe Schillero Jr.

ABOUT THE AUTHOR

Joe Schillero is a graduate of Liberty University and has been teaching and preaching God's Word since 1983. Joe founded Gateway to the Heart Ministries in 2007. It is his passion to see holiness in the lives of Christians in the areas of media discernment. Joe has been married to his wife Carol since 1988. They have 7 grown children and are members of Parkside Church in Cleveland, Ohio.

GATEWAY TO THE HEART MINISTRIES

Garfield Hts., Ohio 44125

www.gatewaytotheheartministries.com

"Getting people to *think about* what they *think about*."